THE HORSE Poster Book

Written by Wendy Allatson

Photographs by Bob Langrish

Quercus

Contents

Andalusian

Vital statistics

Height: 14.3–16 hands
Color: usually **gray** or black, but can be any color except **chestnut**, **skewbald**, and **piebald**
Physique: beautiful head with a slightly "hooked" nose, large, kind eyes, and small ears; strong, arched neck, muscular body with broad back and rounded **hindquarters**; strong legs; thick tail and mane with heavy forelock

The Andalusian or Pure Bred Spanish Horse is poetry in motion. It moves fluidly, with immense elegance and grace. But the Andalusian is not only beautiful to look at, it is also intelligent, affectionate, obedient, and brave. Placid and kind in nature, it gets on well with both people and other horses. Even the stallions are docile and easy to handle. The Andalusian has been **crossed** with many other breeds in an attempt to pass on some of its many qualities. It is one of the founding breeds for the Lipizzaner at the famous Spanish Riding School in Vienna.

Origins

These beautiful horses come from the province of Andalusia in Spain. Their wild ancestors were crossed with horses brought from northern Europe, and later with **Barb** horses brought from North Africa by the Arabs. Despite their gentle nature, for centuries, they were regarded as the ultimate war horse because of their bravery, speed, and agility. But these qualities were nearly lost when they were crossed with heavier breeds. Fortunately, the "pure bred" Andalusian has made a comeback and is now here to stay.

PONY TALE

The Andalusian knows how to play to the crowd and loves ceremonial occasions. Over the centuries, it has been the favorite of many European kings, earning it the nickname "the Horse of Kings," but not just to ride, it also featured in many royal portraits.

Skills

Alert and quick on its feet, the Andalusian is used to herd cattle in Spain, and is also a star in the bullring where it faces the bull with great courage. It works well in many disciplines, including driving, riding, and jumping, and it is good at **dressage**. And of course, its beauty and graceful movements make it a real showstopper at festivals and in the show ring.

Appaloosa

Vital statistics

Height: 14.2–15.2 hands (not under 14 hands)
Color: usually **roan**, but can be any color; their spots form different patterns, such as "leopard" (all over the body) or "blanket" (on the rump)
Physique: small head and long neck; compact body, short, straight back; wispy mane and tail; strong, **hard feet**

Appaloosas are gentle and willing. They are fast, with plenty of stamina, but are also sure-footed—they can stop or turn suddenly on the spot to avoid danger. They make great **cow horses** since they can cover long distances, but also have the speed and agility needed for herding and roping cattle. To rope a steer, the horse has to separate it from the herd and the rider has to throw a lasso round its head or horns. It requires real skill and great teamwork between horse and rider. In other countries, Appaloosas make top sports horses.

Origins

Appaloosas were bred by the Nez Percé (which means "Pierced Nose") Native Americans in the northwest United States from the spotted horses taken to America by the Spanish. They were named "Palouseys" after the Palouse River that flowed through the region, which later became "Appaloosas," the name we know today. The Native Americans were proud that no two horses had the same markings.

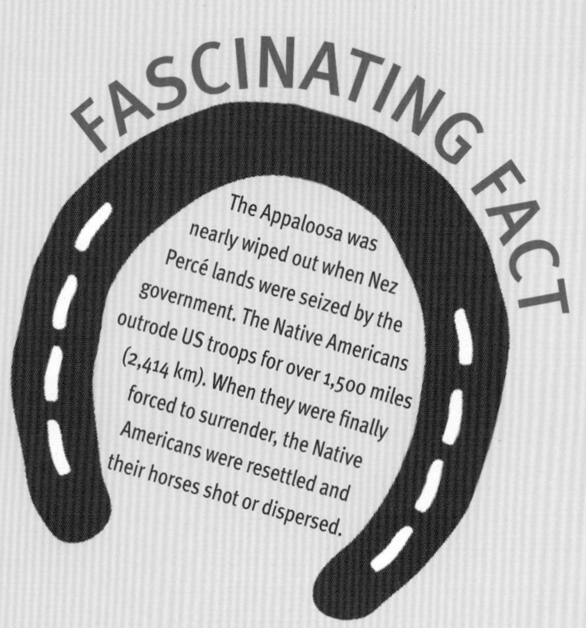

Skills

In the United States, as well as being used as cow horses, Appaloosas star in rodeos, riding, and roping contests. Their graceful movements make them good at **dressage** and give them starring roles in circuses and equestrian shows. They are good jumpers too and, with their sure-footedness and stamina, they make great **endurance** and cross-country horses.

Arab

Vital statistics

Height: 14.2–15.1 hands, but size varies depending on the climate and quality of pasture
Color: **gray**, **chestnut**, and **bay**, but can also be black
Physique: beautiful and graceful; short, fine head, with a curved-in (**dished**) face, flared nostrils and small, pointed ears; elegant, arching neck; compact, well-muscled body with strong **hindquarters**; fine but strong legs

Arab horses are known for their spirited nature, intelligence, and courage. Because of their beauty and graceful movements, they have been **crossed** with breeds throughout the world and most modern breeds have been improved by adding Arab blood. Today, the Arab is found worldwide and many countries have their own breeding programs and produce their own types of Arab. But only Syria has the last descendants of the true desert horses, known as the "Original" or "Elite" Arabs.

Origins

According to one legend, Allah created the horse from a handful of warm wind from the south. Another legend claims that the Arab horse is descended from five mares that were owned by the prophet Muhammad. But legends do sometimes have a grain of truth in them. The Arab came from the windswept deserts of Arabia, and has been bred by the Bedouin tribes of these regions since the time of Muhammad, well over 1,000 years ago. It is thought to be the oldest and purest of all horse breeds. A combination of the Bedouin's breeding skills and the harsh desert climate in which only the strongest can survive, have produced this truly unique horse.

Skills

With its elegant appearance and beautiful, floating action, the Arab is the perfect horse to show in competiton. It is also used in driving events, especially in the United States, while its great energy and stamina make it an ideal **endurance** horse. It can cover distances of between 20 and 110 miles (32 and 177 km), depending on the level of difficulty of the course.

Bashkir Curly

Vital statistics

Height: 13.2–14 hands

Color: usually **chestnut**, but can be **bay** or **buckskin** (dun)

Physique: rather heavy head and short, strong neck; strong, sturdy body with a long, straight back; thick, crinkly mane and tail; short, sturdy legs and small, **hard feet**

In their native Russia, these gentle, good-natured ponies are used for riding, pulling carts, and as a **pack animal.** They are also bred for their milk and meat. The milk is used to make *kumiss*, an alcoholic drink that may not sound very appetizing but is said to be nourishing. Bashkirs are one of the toughest pony breeds. They are used to sub zero temperatures and having to find their food in deep snow. They got their name from their thick, curly winter coat. The hair from the coat is collected and spun to make a warm cloth that is made into clothes and blankets.

Origins

The Bashkir is an ancient breed from Bashkiria, on the Russian steppe (grasslands). It is descended from Przewalski's Horse and the Tarpan, two ancient breeds that gave it its stamina and free, easy movement. There are two types of Bashkir—a smaller mountain pony, which is good for riding, and the steppe pony, which is better for pulling carts. Today, there are around 1,000 Bashkirs (or "Curlies") in the United States, where they were used by Native American tribes in the Northwest, although how they got there is a mystery. Perhaps they crossed from Russia into Alaska via the frozen seas of the Bering Strait?

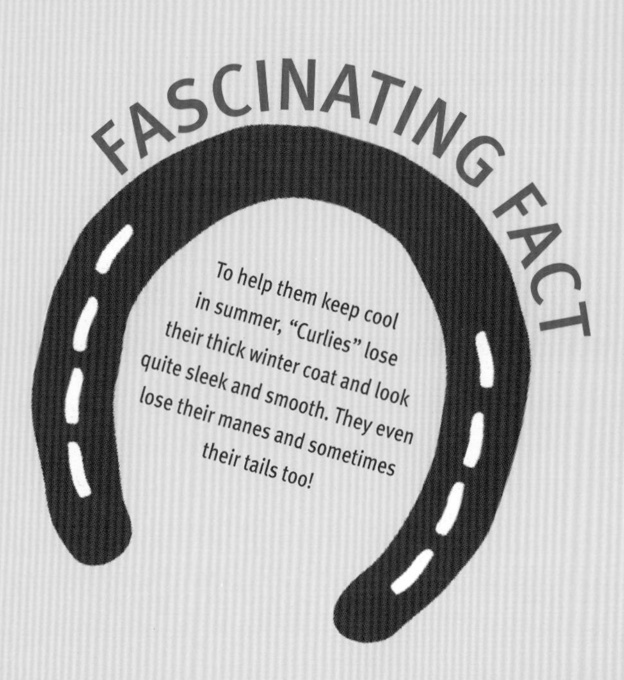

Skills

Bashkirs make good **pleasure** and **harness** ponies. In Russia, their toughness and strength means they can pull sleds for long distances over snow with no extra food. In the United States, they make great **trail** and **endurance** ponies, while their loving nature makes them popular with children.

Clydesdale

Vital statistics

Height: usually about 16.2 hands, but up to 18 hands

Color: mostly **bay** or brown, but also **roan**, **gray**, black, and **chestnut**; lots of white on the face and legs, and sometimes under the body

Physique: broad, flat face with an intelligent eye; long, arched neck, short, strong back and powerful, well-muscled **hindquarters**; long, straight legs with silky **feathers** covering **hard feet**

Like the English Shire Horse, the Clydesdale is brave, gentle, and friendly, but it is lighter and more active than its English cousin. The best examples of the breed are handsome, strong, and powerful, but not too heavy. They have a long, free stride and their **gaits** are amazingly active for such big horses—they pick their feet up cleanly so that anyone walking behind can see the inside of their hooves.

Origins

Clydesdales were bred for farm work in the Scottish region of Clydesdale (now called Lanarkshire). Hardy native mares were crossed with Flemish and Shire stallions in order to increase the Clydesdale's size, and to add to its weight and strength. When road surfaces changed from dirt tracks to hard surfaces made of stone, it meant that heavy loads could be pulled along more easily on carts. Clydesdales then became popular for pulling heavy wagons in towns, and they were exported to other countries such as North and South America, Russia, Australia, and New Zealand. From the 1940s, tractors and trucks began to take over their work, but Clydesdales have recently made a comeback as workhorses, and are also becoming popular as **pleasure horses** and in the show ring.

Skills

Many Clydesdales served in the British army during the First World War. Today, they are used for showing and driving, but also for farm and forestry work (pulling heavy logs), and even for riding. You will certainly have a good view from the back of a mighty Clydesdale. But although big, they certainly aren't slow. Because they pick their feet up well, they are a lively but comfortable ride.

Connemara

Vital statistics

Height: 13–14 hands

Color: usually **gray**, but can be brown, black or **bay**

Physique: a strong, compact body; short legs and **hard feet**; thick mane and tail

Connemaras were originally **buckskin** (dun) with a stripe on their back and black **points**, but this color is now quite rare. Their kind nature and sure-footedness make them a great choice for young riders. Connemaras are tough and hardy. They can live out in all kinds of weather. Like native British ponies, they grow strong and sturdy, even on poor quality grass or pasture. In fact, when lucky enough to graze on rich pasture, Connemaras often grow taller than normal for their breed, and exceed the official height limit of 14.2 hands.

Origins

The Connemara is named after a mountain region in western Ireland. It shares the same Celtic origins as Highland, Icelandic, and Norwegian ponies, but also has **Barb** (North African) and Andalusian (Spanish) blood. According to one legend, when the Spanish Armada, a fleet of Spanish ships sent to attack England, was wrecked off the coast of Ireland in the 1500s, some of the horses on board escaped onto dry land. If they mated with the local Connemaras, this would certainly explain the Spanish part of their ancestry.

Skills

This intelligent, versatile pony is good at a number of different horse disciplines, from hunting to children's competitions. Naturally sure-footed, when crossed with Thoroughbreds, it makes a fast and agile show jumper and is also a great **dressage** pony.

Dartmoor

Vital statistics

Height: up to 12.2 hands

Color: black, brown, or **bay**; **piebald** and **skewbald** exist but are not recognized by the breed society; large amounts of white are frowned upon

Physique: small, noble head with an intelligent eye and small, alert ears; strong, well-muscled back and strong **hindquarters**; strong, slender legs and **hard feet**; full mane and tail

Kind, sensible, and sure-footed, Dartmoors make ideal children's ponies. They are tough and easy to keep. Like other British breeds, such as the Exmoor and Shetland ponies, they live on open moorland where they often have to put up with very harsh conditions. They can survive several feet of snow in winter with no shelter and no extra food.

Origins

For as long as anyone can remember, these tough little ponies have lived on Dartmoor, a large area of moorland in southwest England. Until the late 1800s, the breed was not officially registered, and Dartmoors came in all shapes and sizes. Before then, the moor had provided the pit ponies that were needed to work in the coal mines of North England. Shetland stallions had been allowed to run free and breed with the native moorland ponies. The ponies that were produced as a result were small but strong, just perfect for pulling heavy wagons of coal along miles of narrow tunnels in the mines.

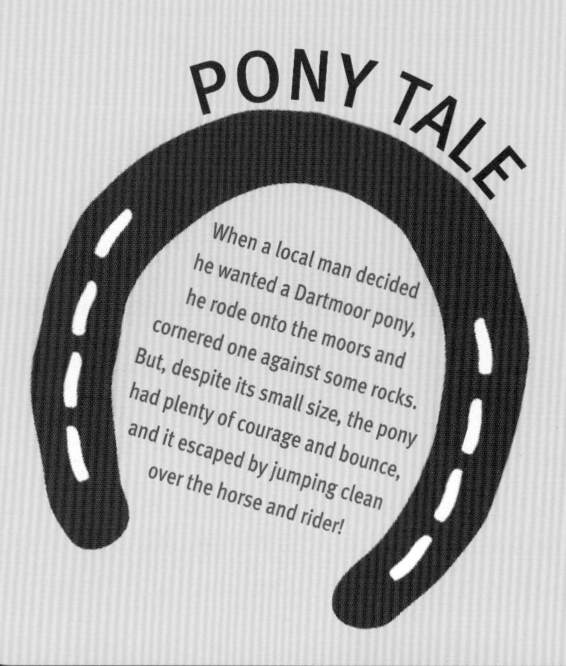

Skills

Dartmoors are good with children. They jump well and like showing off, and they excel in the show ring. They are also good **in harness**—their distinctive appearance makes them easy to match for driving teams, and they certainly stand out from the crowd.

Falabella

Vital statistics

Height: up to 7 hands
Color: all colors, although Appaloosa markings are becoming very popular
Physique: head often quite large in relation to the body and neck developed on the underside ("ewe-necked"); flat **withers**; **hindquarters** tend to drop away; legs may be badly formed and **hocks** weak; mane and tail full and thick, like the Shetland's

This horse was first bred by the Falabella family on their ranch near Buenos Aires, in Argentina. It is also known as the Miniature Horse in the United States and the Toy Horse in Britain. It is the smallest horse in the world, but is still regarded as a horse rather than a pony. Ponies have been bred in harsh conditions that have stunted their growth, so their legs may look a little too short or their heads a little too large for their bodies. However, the Falabella is in perfect proportion and, as its name suggests, looks more like a miniature horse.

Origins

Although the breed is less than 100 years old, there are no records of its early development. It is descended from a small Thoroughbred owned by the Falabella family that was **crossed** with small Shetlands. When the smallest of these first crosses were then interbred, the Falabella "shrank" even further, and the result was the perfect miniature horse. Unfortunately, inbreeding often causes problems such as heavy heads, crooked legs, and weak hocks, and Falabellas sometimes suffer from such problems.

Skills

These tiny horses are popular in North America for use **in harness**, but they are not strong enough to be used as riding ponies, even for tiny children. They are about the same size as a big dog, such as a Great Dane. Friendly, intelligent, and full of character, Falabellas enjoy being around people and so make ideal pets or companions.

Fjord

Vital statistics

Height: 13–14.2 hands

Color: **buckskin** (dun), usually cream or yellow, with a stripe on its back and sometimes striped forelegs and inner thighs; black and silver tail and mane

Physique: small head with wide-set eyes and small ears; short, thick neck with an upright mane; strong muscular body, long back, and rounded **hindquarters**; short sturdy legs with **feathers** on the heels

The Fjord (or Westlands) pony is the oldest and purest of the pony breeds. In fact, it doesn't look much different from the stocky ponies that were used by the Vikings over 1,000 years ago. The Fjord is attractive, a willing worker, kind, and even-tempered. Its gentle nature and the fact that it loves company make it easy to handle and fun to be around. Because it is used to the harsh climate of Scandinavia, it is also tough. It is quite easy to keep since it will munch happily on poor quality grass and doesn't mind the cold.

Origins

The Fjord pony is descended from the wild horses of Russia and Mongolia, and has lived in Norway for almost 2,000 years. The Vikings used it as a war pony, for general transport, and even for horse-fighting—two stallions fought each other, while their owners cheered them on. More recently, these sure-footed, hardy ponies have been used as work ponies and **pack animals**. Today they are still found pulling plows and carts, and carrying loads along mountain paths that are too steep or narrow for tractors and trucks. The Fjord is bred widely throughout Norway and is also very popular in Sweden and Denmark.

Skills

Fjords make great work ponies and are also ideal for driving, **trail riding**, and **endurance**. They're pretty good at mounted games too. But be warned—they have a reputation for developing "attitude" if they're not ridden often enough. So if your Fjord is being a little stubborn, the secret is to be tactful and kind, but firm.

Friesian

Friesian

Vital statistics

Height: 15–16 hands
Color: black with no markings of any kind
Physique: long, narrow head with short, pointed ears and a kind eye; long, arching neck; short, strong back and rounded **hindquarters**; strong, sturdy legs with **feathers** on the heels; thick, wavy mane and tail

The Friesian is very kind and gentle. Thanks to its sturdy ancestors, it is tough and strong, while its **Barb** blood gives it spirit, stamina, and endurance. Its beautiful high-stepping action and free, easy movement come from its Andalusian ancestors. There are more than 30,000 Friesians registered worldwide, but in the United States and Canada they are quite rare, numbering only 1–2,000.

Origins

Friesians come from the province of Friesland in the Netherlands and are descended from the Forest Horse that roamed northern Europe in prehistoric times. They were used as heavy riding horses and war horses during the Middle Ages, when knights in heavy armor needed horses with size, strength, and stamina. They were **crossed** with Barbs from the East, and North Africa, during the Crusades. The more elegant Friesian that is lighter in weight was produced when it was crossed with the Andalusian from Spain.

Skills

Unfortunately, the Friesian's role as a **draft** and workhorse was threatened when the breed became lighter in weight and the automobile was invented. Today, however, the lighter-weight Friesian with its beautiful movement, good looks, and proud bearing makes a great carriage and **dressage** horse. It is also popular in circuses and equestrian shows, where it is used for riding displays and as a liberty horse (one that performs without a rider or reins).

Haflinger

Vital statistics

Height: 14 hands
Color: **chestnut** with a flaxen mane and tail, other colors are very rare
Physique: slightly pointed face, kind eye, and small ears; strong, muscular body with a broad chest, long, broad back and strong **hindquarters**; short sturdy legs and **hard feet**

Haflinger ponies are bred on mountain pastures where they roam free for the first four years of their life before being **broken in**. They may be late starters, but they live for a long time and some are still working at the ripe old age of 40! Like most pony breeds, Haflingers have adapted to the extreme conditions of their native country—they are strong, tough, and sure-footed, which makes them well suited to mountain regions. And like most ponies, they don't mind the cold and do well on poor-quality grass or pasture. They will live out happily in all kinds of weather with some form of shelter and just a little extra food!

Origins

The Haflinger is an ancient breed that comes from the southern Tyrolean Mountains, in what is now Austria and Northern Italy, where it is known to have lived since medieval times. It is named after the Austrian village of Hafling (which became part of Italy in 1919) and is descended from Austrian heavy horses like the Noriker. Arab blood was introduced in the 1800s, when Haflinger mares were **crossed** with the half-Arab stallion "El Bedavi." Today, breeding is carefully controlled by the state **studs**.

Skills

In the past, Haflingers were used as **pack** and **draft** animals, and they are still used today for forestry work in the high mountains. Their free, easy movement and long, smooth stride make them great to ride or drive, and they do well in **dressage**, show jumping and **harness** competitions. Hardy and sure-footed, they are also ideal for **trail riding** and **endurance** riding, while their kind nature makes them a popular choice for disabled rider programs.

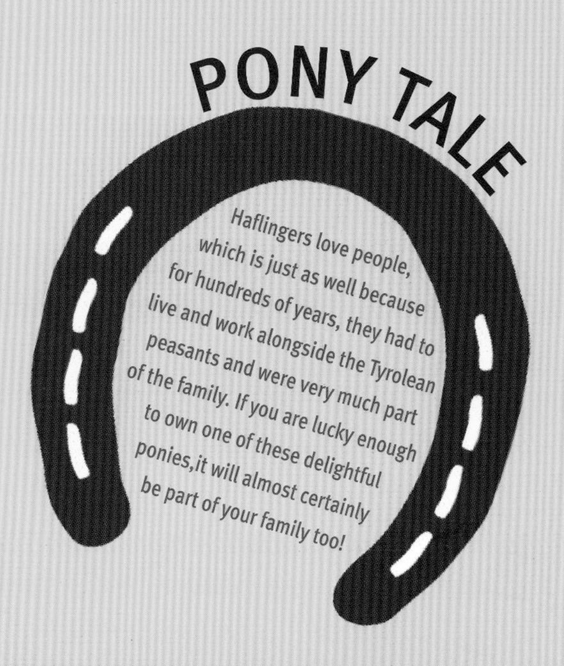

Icelandic

Vital statistics

Height: 12–13 hands
Color: mostly **gray**, **buckskin** (dun), but also **chestnut**, **bay**, brown, black, gray, **palomino**, and sometimes **piebald** and **skewbald**
Physique: large head, broad forehead, and intelligent eye; short, muscular neck on a short, stocky body; broad, short **hindquarters**; short, sturdy legs; thick mane and tail

The Icelandic pony is one of the toughest pony breeds since it lives in harsh, almost arctic conditions. It is usually friendly and obedient but, like most small ponies, can sometimes be a little stubborn. Until quite recently, Iceland had few tracks or roads that were suitable for motor vehicles, so these ponies were used as **pack animals** and for getting around. They are very comfortable to ride since, as well as the usual speeds of walk, trot, and canter, they have an extra **gait**—a pace called the "tölt." This fast, extended trot allows the rider to sit quite still in the saddle, even though they are traveling almost as fast as at a canter!

Origins

The first ponies were brought to Iceland around 870 by Norwegian settlers who wanted to escape their unpopular king, Harold Fairhair. They were **crossed** with Celtic ponies brought in by other settlers—Shetland and Highland ponies from Scotland and the Connemara from Ireland—and the result was the Icelandic pony. The introduction of breeds from other countries was banned, so the breed has remained pure for the last 1,000 years. Until the 1900s, Icelandic ponies were exported to Britain for use as pack and **draft** animals, and to work in the coal mines.

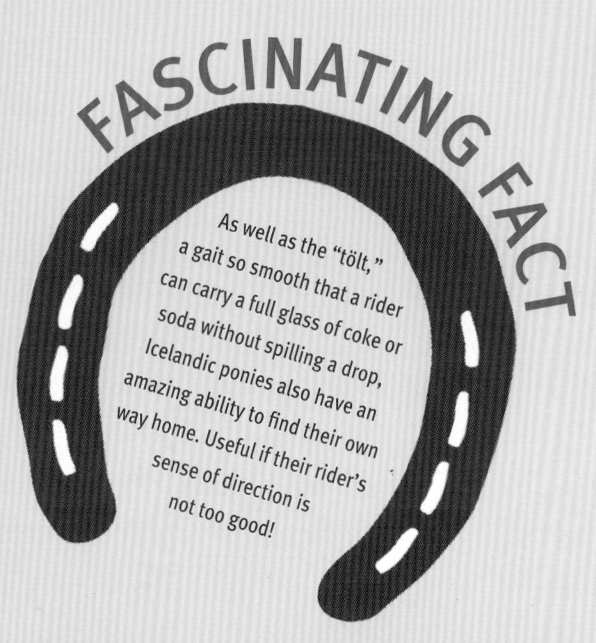

Skills

In Iceland, these ponies are still used as pack animals, for herding sheep, and for generally getting around. They make great driving and riding ponies, and although quite small, their strong, muscular bodies make them ideal mounts for both children and adults.

Irish Draught Sport Horse

Vital statistics

Height: 16–16.3 hands

Color: any **solid color**

Physique: good-looking **hunter**/show jumper **type**; Thoroughbred-type head with an alert expression; good shoulders, and a big, broad chest; strong **hindquarters**; strong, hard legs and good, **hard feet**

The Irish Draught Sport Horse is a type rather than a breed. The "Sport Horse" part of the name shows its type (it is used for sports) and "Irish Draught" shows that it was bred from the Irish Draught Horse. Today, the Irish Draught Sport Horse is well known as a show jumper and an **eventer**, but it was originally bred for hunting with hounds. Because of its hunting background, it is bold and intelligent. It is also good tempered and has excellent manners, both of which are important qualities for a hunter.

Origins

The Irish Draught Sport Horse is a **cross** between the slightly heavier Irish Draught Horse and the Thoroughbred—or any other good-quality lightweight horse. This cross produces the famous Irish hunters and jumpers that combine the stamina and power of the Irish Draught with the speed and agility of the Thoroughbred. Irish-bred **pleasure horses**, racehorses, and show jumpers, are famous for their quality and are found throughout the world.

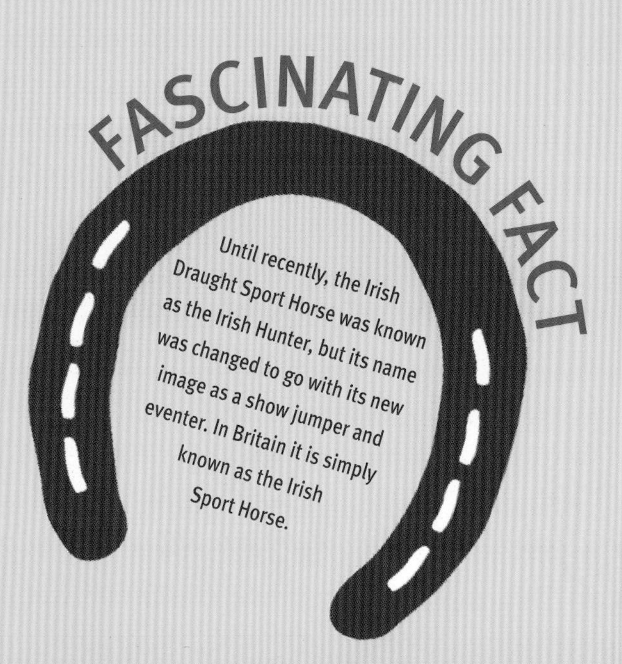

Skills

The Irish Draught Sport Horse is a great all-rounder. It does well in the **dressage** ring and is a bold jumper, whether in the show ring, or when tackling ditches or walls when being ridden across country. Thanks to these skills, many of these horses are top show jumpers and eventers, winning medals and rosettes galore in competitions all over the world.

Lipizzaner

Vital statistics

Height: 15–16 hands
Color: mostly **gray** (white) but can also be black, **bay** or **chestnut**
Physique: straight face, strong, arched neck, long back, well-muscled shoulders and strong legs

Lipizzaner foals have dark gray or black coats, which become gradually lighter as they get older, and turn white when they are fully grown. Often capable of working for 25–30 years, they are extremely intelligent, even-tempered, and obedient. Because of their beautiful physique and good nature, they are used for the precision **dressage** displays of the Spanish Riding School of Vienna in Austria (so-called because it only uses "Spanish" horses). However, only the stallions are strong enough to perform the very difficult movements (called **high-school** movements) that have made the school famous throughout the world.

Origins

The breed was developed in Austria over 400 hundred years ago by Archduke Charles II, the son of the Austrian emperor. He imported a total of 9 stallions and 24 mares from Spain. Lipizzaners are named after the famous **stud** at Lipica, founded in 1580, where these beautiful animals were first bred. Today, Lipizzaners are still bred at Lipica (which is now in Slovenia) and also at the Piber stud in Austria, where they were **crossed** with several other breeds, including the Arab.

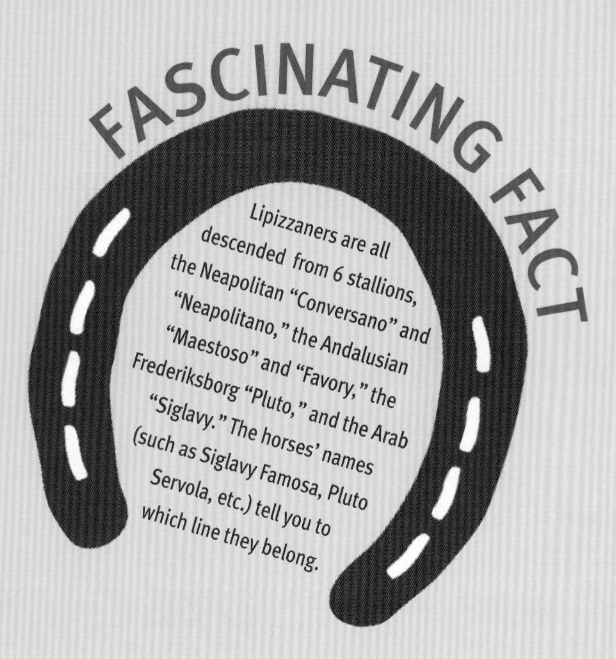

Skills

The Lipizzaner's obedient nature and breeding makes it a wonderful dressage horse, but it takes 5 years of training, and the stallions chosen have to be strong enough to perform such demanding movements as the *levade*, a half-rear where the horse balances and supports the weight of its body (and its rider!) on its **hindquarters**.

Lusitano

Vital statistics

Height: 15–16 hands

Color: usually **gray**, but can be any **solid color**

Physique: smallish head, with a straight face and small ears; muscular neck, compact body, and strong, rounded **hindquarters**; long, fine legs; wavy mane and tail

There have been Lusitanos in Portugal for hundreds of years. The family resemblance to its Spanish cousin, the Andalusian, is strong. They are very similar in both looks and character. Like its cousin, the Lusitano is intelligent, obedient, and brave. Both horses have a beautiful, floating style and flowing movements, and are really good at **dressage**. And just like the Andalusian, the Lusitano's speed and agility made it popular as a cavalry horse, and also in the bullring where it can still be seen today.

Origins

The Lusitano and Andalusian share the same ancestors and, until fairly recently, were regarded as two branches (Portuguese and Spanish) of the same family. Their proud bearing made them the favorites of many European kings, until the sport of horse racing became popular and the swift Arab and English Thoroughbreds took their place as royal favorites. Luckily, they became fashionable again and the Portuguese horse was given its own identity. Today it is known as the Lusitano or Pure Bred Lusitano.

Skills

The Lusitano has similar skills to the Andalusian. Agile and intelligent, it excels in the bullring where its ability to spring forward powerfully and suddenly helps keep it out of trouble. The Lusitano is also a great performer, and its graceful, flowing movements are amazing to watch—in the dressage arena, at the circus, or in shows. But the Lusitano doesn't always have to be in front of a crowd, it is a good horse to ride for pleasure too.

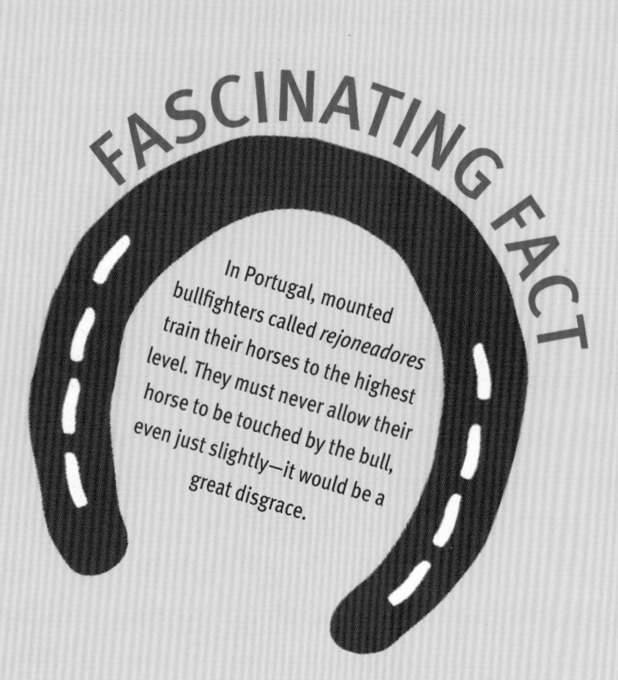

Missouri Foxtrotter

Missouri Foxtrotter

Vital statistics

Height: 16–17 hands
Color: usually **chestnut**, but can be any color
Physique: neat, intelligent head with pointed ears; longish neck and powerful shoulders; short back with well-developed **hindquarters**; strong legs and feet

The Missouri Foxtrotter is an American **gaited** horse. It has an unusual natural gait, a pace called a "walking trot." It walks with its front legs while trotting with its hind legs! This strange gait is very comfortable for the rider as the horse's back moves very little, unlike in the normal trot. It enables the horse and rider to travel for long distances at a speed of around 5 miles/8 km an hour (about the speed of a normal trot) and twice as fast over short distances.

Origins

The Foxtrotter was bred in the United States in the early 1800s by settlers in Arkansas and Missouri. The settlers spent long hours in the saddle, and so wanted a hardy, sure-footed horse that was comfortable to ride for long distances over rough ground. They **crossed** Morgans with Thoroughbreds and the descendants of the Spanish-**Barb** horses brought in by Spanish explorers in the 1500s. The results of these crosses were then crossed again, this time with American **gaited** horses (Saddlebreds and Tennessee Walking Horses), and the Missouri Foxtrotter was finally born.

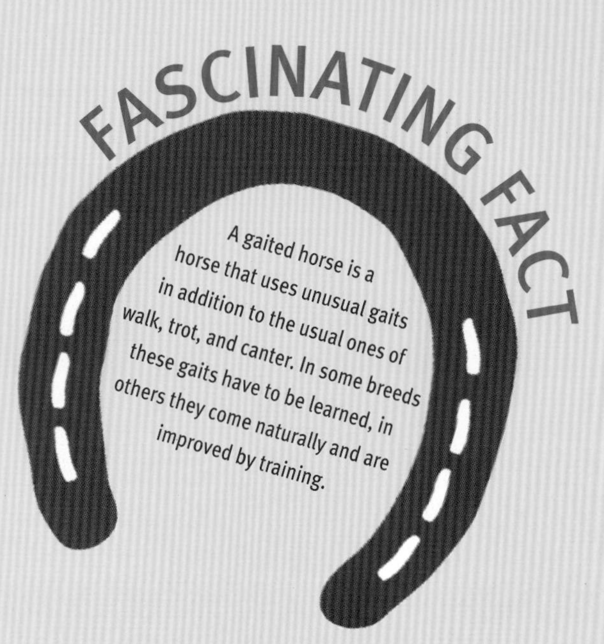

Skills

Foxtrotters were bred to be comfortable, long-distance **saddle horses** and today are popular as **pleasure** and **trail-riding** horses. They are also bred for the show ring. True to their American pioneer heritage, they are usually ridden and are always shown in competitions in a Western saddle and bridle.

Morgan

Vital statistics

Height: 14.2–15.2 hands

Color: usually, **bay**, dark brown, or **chestnut**, but can be any **solid color** except **gray**

Physique: short, broad head with small ears and a kind eye; thick, muscular neck and strong shoulders; short, muscular body and strong, well-formed **hindquarters**; strong legs; thick mane and tail

Morgans are hardy horses with great strength and stamina. The ordinary Morgan is stocky and muscular, but the show Morgan is taller and finer and holds its head and tail higher. Like the American Saddlebred, its feet are left to grow long and are shod with heavy horseshoes to improve its action in the show ring. But whatever they are used for, whether it is for work, to show, or for play, Morgans are spirited and intelligent horses that are good-natured, friendly, and easy to manage. They are a pleasure to be around.

Origins

All Morgans are descended from the same ancestor, a stallion originally called "Figure" and later renamed "Justin Morgan," after his owner. "Justin Morgan" (the horse!) was famous for his amazing strength and stamina. After a hard day's work pulling a plow and hauling timber, he still had enough energy to win weight-pulling contests and **harness** and **saddle** races. "Justin Morgan's" own ancestry is a real mystery. According to one story, his father was a Thoroughbred called "True Briton," but according to another, it was a Friesian stallion, while a third story claims he was the son of a Welsh Cob.

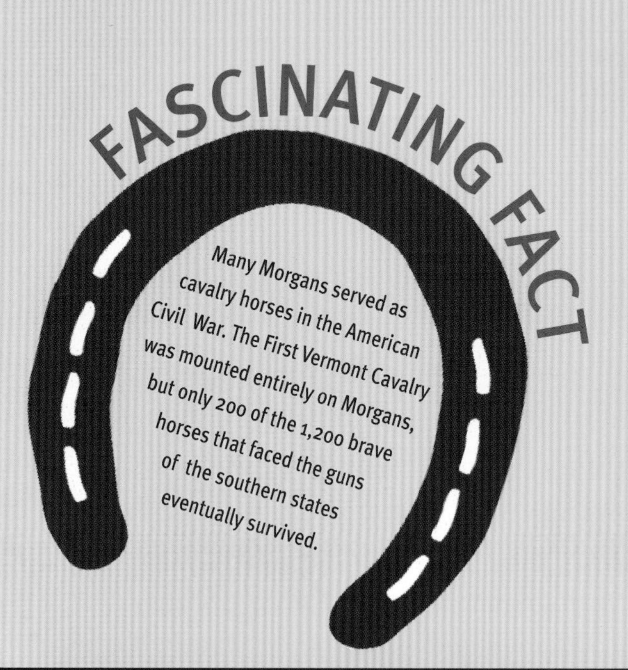

FASCINATING FACT

Many Morgans served as cavalry horses in the American Civil War. The First Vermont Cavalry was mounted entirely on Morgans, but only 200 of the 1,200 brave horses that faced the guns of the southern states eventually survived.

Skills

Today, the Morgan is still used for farm work and as a **cow horse** in the United States, where it is also an all-round **pleasure horse**. It is great for driving and riding, and is especially popular for **trail** and **endurance** riding. A finer, slightly taller type of Morgan is bred for the show ring.

Mustang

Mustang

Vital statistics

Height: 13.2–15 hands, usually 14.2 hands
Color: full range of coat colors
Physique: strong, wiry body; hard, strong legs and tough, **hard feet** that don't need shoes; thick mane and tail

Mustangs come in all shapes, sizes, and colors. They are tough, wiry, and hardy, and are also very fast and sure-footed. In the early 1900s, there were around 2 million Mustangs in the Western United States, but, by 1926 this number had been reduced by half. As the settlers moved West, they needed to find land for their cattle and sheep. Much of it was grazed by wild Mustangs and some ranchers simply shot them on sight to clear the land for their livestock. Mustangs are now protected by law and there are special areas where they can roam freely and safely. Today, there are over 40,000 Mustangs in the American West.

Origins

Mustangs are descended from the horses brought to South America by the Spanish in the 1500s. The name comes from the Spanish word *mesteño* meaning "stray horse." Some of these Spanish horses were turned loose or escaped and roamed wild, spreading into North America and onto the western plains. In order to survive, they had to adapt to their new surroundings. Gradually, over the years, these good-quality Spanish horses were transformed into fairly ordinary but very tough ponies. Some of these ponies were used by the Native Americans, others became the first **cow ponies**. Some Mustangs were even **crossed** with other horses to produce new breeds like the Chickasaw Native American Pony and the Quarter Horse.

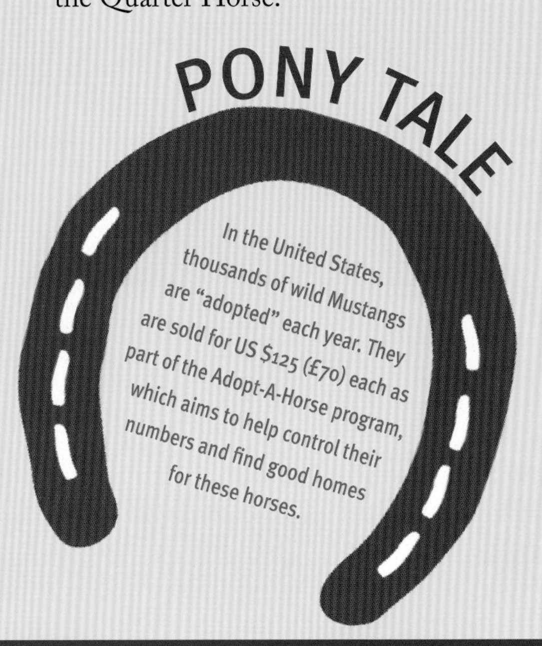

PONY TALE

In the United States, thousands of wild Mustangs are "adopted" each year. They are sold for US $125 (£70) each as part of the Adopt-A-Horse program, which aims to help control their numbers and find good homes for these horses.

Skills

The Mustang is best known as the famous "bucking bronco." Some are still used and are even specially bred for rodeos, where they also compete in other riding events. But if they are properly trained, they make good cow ponies and riding ponies, while their stamina makes them great for **trail riding**.

Paint Horse

Vital statistics

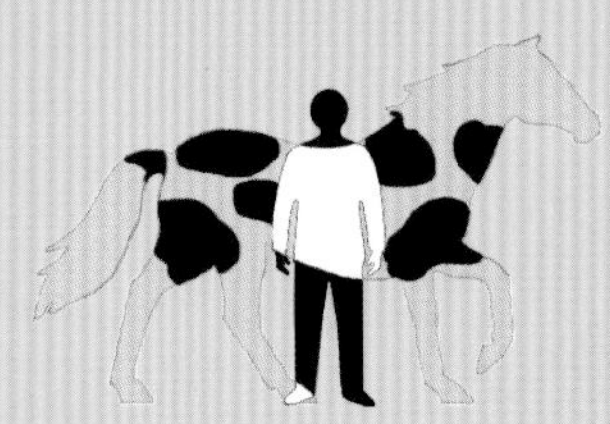

Height: 15–16 hands

Color: **piebald** (black and white) and **skewbald** (white and any other color except black)

Physique: Paint Horses have Quarter Horse or Thoroughbred ancestry so their physique varies—usually a short, pretty head and long, muscular neck; short back and powerful **hindquarters**; most have strong legs and feet

Don't confuse the Paint Horse with the Pinto. Although both names come from the Spanish *pintado* meaning "painted," they are not the same breed. They are both "colored" horses and both have a particular type of coloring—tobiano or overo. Tobianos have large patches of black, brown, or red on a white coat, while overos have white patches on a dark coat. The difference is that any breed of horse that has this kind of coloring can be called a Pinto (e.g. an overo Paso Fino is also a Pinto), but the Paint Horse is a breed in its own right. Paints are known as Coloureds in Britain.

Origins

Like most American breeds, the Paint Horse is descended from the horses brought to America by the Spanish in the 1500s. Some of these horses escaped or strayed and joined the wild herds that roamed the western plains. Some were tamed and became Native American ponies or were used as **cow ponies**. Over the years, these horses have been **crossed** with other breeds such as the Quarter Horse and Thoroughbred to improve their physique and athletic skills.

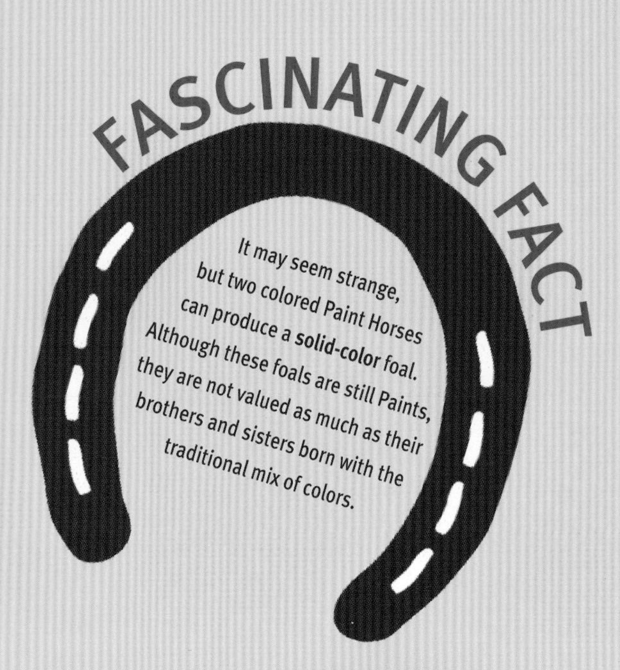

Skills

Paints are still used on ranches as cow ponies—they are even-tempered, fast, quick on their feet, and really good at cutting (separating one cow from the herd) and herding cattle. They also compete in rodeos where they star in penning (separating and driving cows into a pen), cutting, and roping events. As well as being a good choice for children due to their friendly nature, they also make great **pleasure horses** and are very popular for **trail riding**.

Paso Fino

Vital statistics

Height: 14–15 hands

Color: all colors

Physique: Arab-type head with small, pricked ears and an expressive eye; short back with strong **hindquarters**; strong legs and **hard feet**; a very tough breed

The Paso Fino got its name from its unusual natural **gait**, which is known as the *paso* (it means "pace" in Spanish). A Paso horse moves its front legs in an outward, circular action (a bit like doing the breast stroke!) rather than backward and forward like most horses. At the same time, it moves its hind legs in a straight line, with its **hindquarters** low and its **hocks** well under its body. This pace comes naturally and does not have to be learned and Paso foals can use it soon after they are born. Training will improve it even more. Pasos love people and are willing and eager to please.

Origins

The Paso Fino comes from Central and South America and the Caribbean. It is similar to the Peruvian Paso (or Stepping Horse) and both breeds are descended from the gaited horses (horses with extra or unusual paces) that were brought to South America by the Spanish in the 1500s. Great care has been taken by breeders over the years to improve the Paso's unusual gait. And today, a special American version of the Paso Fino is being developed in the United States by **cross-breeding** different strains of the South American Paso Fino.

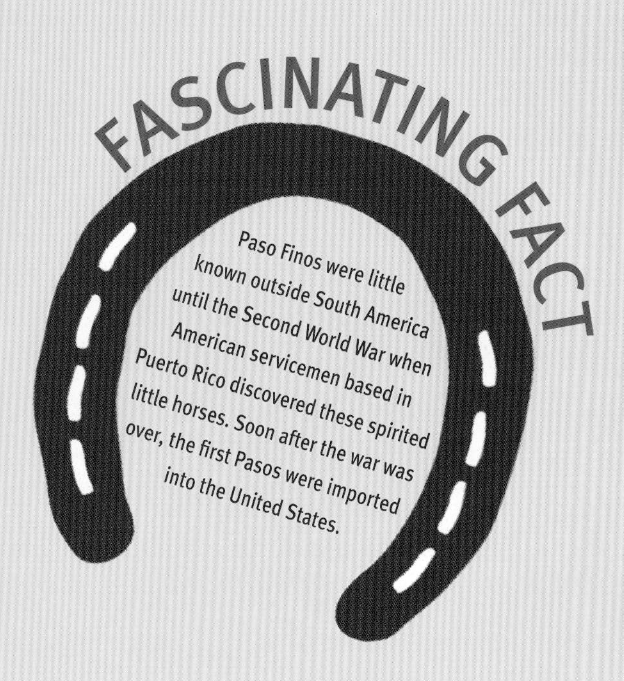

Skills

Thanks to the fact that they are comfortable to ride over long distances, Pasos are used on ranches in South America. They are also becoming increasingly popular as **saddle horses** in the United States, where they make great **trail** horses. They are also in great demand at shows where they make an eye-catching spectacle, with their riders dressed in the national costume of their country of origin, such as Peru or Puerto Rico. They are intelligent and extremely quick to learn.

Percheron

Vital statistics

Height: 15.2–17.2 hands
Color: any shades of **gray** or black
Physique: fine head with a straight face, long ears, and large eyes set wide apart; strong, muscular neck; powerful chest and strong, compact body; very strong, rounded **hindquarters**; solid, muscular legs with some **feathers**

Percherons are intelligent and full of energy. They are also gentle, kind, and easy to handle. Despite their large size and strength, they are elegant, with a long, floating stride. They are often described as "overgrown Arabs" because of their graceful movements. These gentle giants are easy to care for and keep fit and healthy on a simple diet. When it comes to heavy horses, Percherons are the real stars of the show.

Origins

Percherons come from the Perche region of Normandy, in France. They are descended from heavy Norman horses that were **crossed** with Arabs centuries ago. In the Middle Ages, these Norman-Arab crosses carried knights into battle. In France, only horses bred within the Perche region itself are allowed to be called true Percherons, but they are also bred in other parts of the world. They are very popular in the United States, and in Britain, they have been crossed with Thoroughbreds to produce heavy hunters, which can cross fields thick with mud without tiring too quickly.

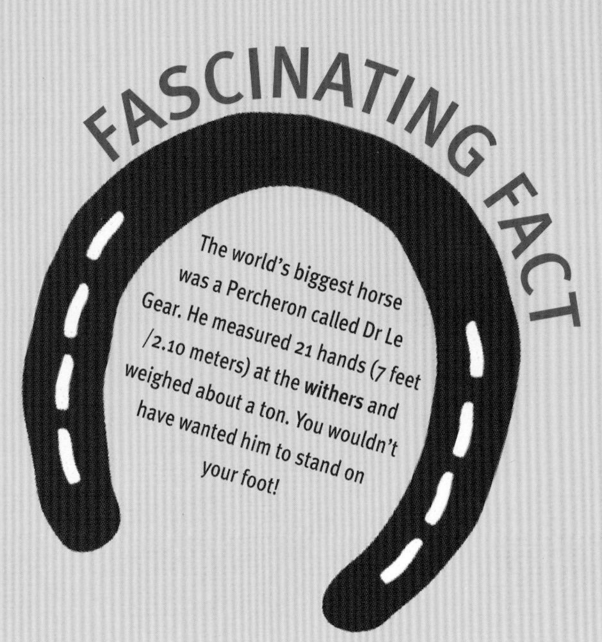

Skills

In the past, Percherons were used as war horses, farm horses, and cart horses. Today, they make beautiful carriage horses and often appear at horse shows, where they are entered in competitions in hand (led in a halter), **in harness** (pulling a cart), and under saddle (with a rider). They are also popular in circuses as their wide, flat backs are ideal for bareback riding.

Pony of the Americas

Vital statistics

Height: 11.2–13 hands
Color: Appaloosa, with any of the Appaloosa color patterns
Physique: Arab head with a curved-in (**dished**) face, large eyes and pointed ears; slightly arching neck, short, muscular back, and well-muscled **hindquarters**; strong legs and good **hard feet**

The Pony of the Americas (POA), which looks like a miniature Appaloosa, is one of the newest pony breeds. It is very willing and gentle, and its kind nature and good manners, along with its smooth stride, make it a good choice for children. The POA also helps to give the rider confidence because it seems to sense what is being asked of it and does its best to please.

Origins

The POA was created in Iowa in the United States, in 1956, when a Shetland stallion was **crossed** with an Appaloosa mare. The result was a miniature Appaloosa colt (a male foal), named "Black Hand" because of the dark, hand-like markings on its back. "Black Hand" was such a hit in the show ring that he was used to found this new breed, which has also been crossed with Arabs, Quarter Horses, and Welsh ponies. By the late 1990s, there were 40,000 registered POAs (those whose parentage can be listed in the official breed registry) in the United States, compared with just 12,000 in the 1970s, an increase that shows just how successful these delightful ponies have been.

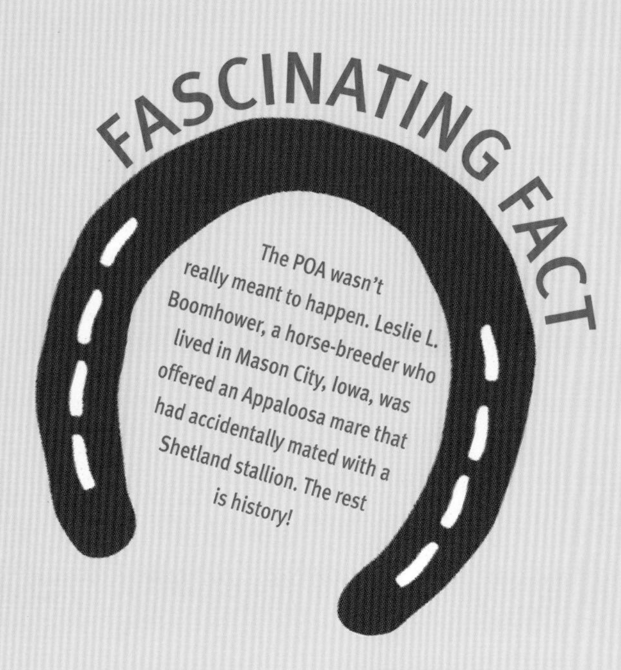

Skills

The POA is a good all-rounder. It is a popular **pleasure pony** and is great for **trail** and **endurance** riding. It loves to compete and is good at show jumping and children's races. Its attractive markings make it a winner in the show ring, where it competes in classes in hand (led in a halter) and **in harness** (pulling a cart).

Quarter Horse

Vital statistics

Height: 15–16 hands

Color: all **solid colors** but mainly **sorrel** (reddish chestnut)

Physique: small head, broad forehead, and kind eyes; muscular neck, short, muscular back, and powerful, rounded **hindquarters**; fine legs for such a powerful body

The Quarter Horse is the oldest of the American breeds. Intelligent, gentle, and eager to please, it always does its best to do what its rider asks. The Quarter Horse is good at lots of different horse disciplines and is the most popular breed in the world. It is extremely fast over short distances and can even outrun a Thoroughbred over a short course.

Origins

Quarter Horses are descended from heavy English workhorses brought to Virginia and Carolina by English settlers in the 1600s. These horses were **crossed** with swift Native American ponies to produce fast, powerful horses used for farm work, herding cattle, pulling wagons, and for riding. They were also ridden in races run over courses a quarter of a mile (400 meters) long. The races became very popular, and so the horses were named "quarter horses" after them. The Quarter Horse's powerful hindquarters give it tremendous powers of acceleration. It can leap straight to a gallop from a standstill!

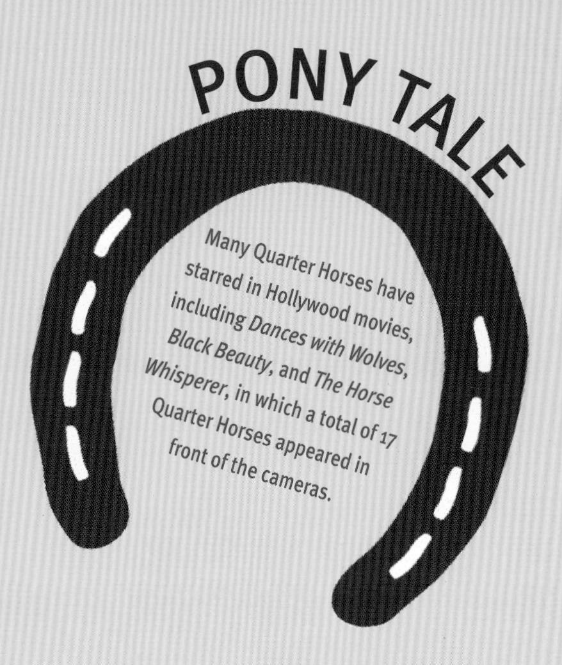

Skills

Quarter Horses are said to have a real gift for herding cattle, and they are still used as **cow horses** in the United States, where they make great ranch and rodeo horses. They are nimble and quick, and can turn on the spot in a flash. They can race and jump, and perform well at **dressage**, and are a favorite for **trail riding**.

Saddlebred

Vital statistics

Height: 15–16 hands

Color: usually black, brown, **bay**, or **chestnut**; often white markings on the face and legs

Physique: small head with a straight face and alert eye, carried high on an arched neck; short, well-muscled body and strong, flexible **hindquarters**; fine, elegant legs; feet usually left to grow long and shod with heavy shoes; full mane and tail, carried high

The American Saddlebred (or Kentucky Saddler) was bred in the southern United States as a comfortable riding horse for plantation owners. Today, it is used mainly in the show ring. When due to be shown, its feet are left to grow long and are shod with heavier horseshoes than normal. This helps to improve its movements. The American Saddlebred is called a five-**gaited** horse, which means it has five paces. It lifts its legs very high when it walks, trots, and canters, but it also has a slow, prancing pace called the "slow gait," where it almost looks as though it is dancing, and a much faster, running pace called the "rack."

Origins

The Saddlebred was developed in the 1800s by crossing two gaited breeds—the Narragansett Pacer, a plantation workhorse that no longer exists as a breed, and the Canadian Pacer. The first Saddlebreds were then crossed again with Morgans and Thoroughbreds, which gave them extra speed, beautiful movements, and more style and elegance. Saddlebreds are spirited but are also friendly and are very willing workers.

Skills

The Saddlebred is a very showy, eye-catching horse. Whether it is ridden or driven **in harness**, it is just perfect for the show ring, where it performs with the elegance of a ballet dancer. When its feet are trimmed and shod normally, the Saddlebred makes a great **pleasure horse**, and it is popular for **trail riding**, jumping, and driving.

Selle Français (French Saddle Horse)

Vital statistics

Height: 15.2–16.3 hands

Color: any **solid color**, but usually **chestnut**

Physique: broad head with long ears and eyes set wide apart; long, strong neck, long back and rounded **hindquarters**; long, muscular legs

The Selle Français or French Saddle Horse is a **type** rather than a breed, and is a newcomer to the world of official horse breeds as it was only named a breed in 1958. In fact, it is a new, improved version of the Anglo-Norman, which was itself an improvement on the Norman saddle horse. Today, the Selle Français is **crossed** with the Thoroughbred (for its speed and mental agility) and the Arab (for its spirit and stamina). Although the Selle Français is still bred in Normandy, other French regions are starting to breed them too.

Origins

The heavy Norman horse that lived in France 1,000 years ago was used as a **saddle horse** and war horse. It went out of style when war horses needed to be faster and lighter, but was still used as a **draft** and workhorse. Norman mares were crossed with lighter horses with stamina, and produced a new type of Norman saddle horse. This saddle horse was then crossed with English Thoroughbreds and Trotters to create the Anglo-Norman. After the Second World War, French breeders crossed the Anglo-Norman with other French breeds, but these horses began to look so much alike that it was decided to call them all the Selle Français.

Skills

The Selle Français is still used as a cavalry horse by the Swiss army. It is very athletic and competes in a wide range of horse disciplines. It is skilled at **dressage** and show jumping, as well as cross-country and **endurance** riding, and makes a great three-day **eventer**. It is considered one of the world's finest sports horses.

Shetland

Vital statistics

Height: 9.3–10.2 hands; the smallest Shetland ever stood 6.2 hands—26 inches (66 cm) high!

Color: black or dark brown but can be any color, including **piebald** and **skewbald**

Physique: small head with large, kind eyes and small ears; thick mane and tail (often touching the ground); short, strong back and short, sturdy legs

Shetlands are small, cuddly ponies with a gentle nature and a sense of humor. They are also very hardy as they come from the cold, windswept islands of northern Scotland. Their thick winter coat means they can live out in all weathers, and they graze happily on poor pasture. The American Shetland is taller (up to 11.2 hands) and less chunky than its Scottish cousin, and has been bred for the show ring. Some owners add false tails and hooves to "improve" its appearance when it is being shown.

Origins

The Shetland has lived on the Orkney and Shetland Islands for centuries. It is not known exactly how it got there, but it was probably brought in from Europe, where Shetland-type ponies can be seen in ancient cave paintings. Due to the harsh conditions of northern Scotland, with its cold climate and poor pasture, Shetlands had little chance of growing tall and probably even got smaller on their diet of poor grass. They were not usually ridden due to their small size, but were used as **pack animals**, and were perfect for working in mines. Modern Shetlands are descended from the ponies that were bred to work in English coal mines in the 1800s.

Skills

These sure-footed, tough little ponies are still used to carry loads on the Shetland Islands, but they are also popular as **pleasure ponies** in Europe and the United States. Their small size makes them ideal first ponies for children, and they also work well when driven. They are still in demand for circus work thanks to their appealing character and cute looks.

Tennessee
Walking Horse

Tennessee Walking Horse

Vital statistics

Height: 15–17 hands

Color: any **solid color**

Physique: plain head with alert ears, carried on a strong, arched neck; broad, powerful body with strong **hindquarters**; strong legs; thick mane and tail, usually worn long, with a high tail carriage

The Tennessee Walking Horse is slightly heavier than its cousin, the Saddlebred. Like its cousin, it is also a **gaited** horse but has three, rather than five gaits or paces—a flat walk, a running walk, which is very comfortable for both the horse and its rider, and a smooth, rocking canter. In the running walk, the horse looks as though it is gliding along the ground. It also nods its head in time with its feet, which is special to the Walker. These horses are intelligent, kind, and willing. It is thought that they are the most naturally good-tempered of all horse breeds.

Origins

The Tennessee Walker was developed in the 1800s by the plantation owners of Tennessee, who spent many hours in the saddle and wanted a strong horse that was also comfortable to ride. Like the Saddlebred, the Tennessee Walker is descended from the Narragansett Pacer and has been **crossed** with several other breeds. Like the Morgan, it can trace its ancestry back to just one stallion—a small, black Standardbred named "Black Allen," which had a peculiar running walk. He was bought at the ripe old age of 23 by Albert Dement of Wartrace, Tennessee, who wanted to produce a breed that could do the running walk naturally. Albert had made a good buy, and Tennessee Walkers have been using the running walk ever since.

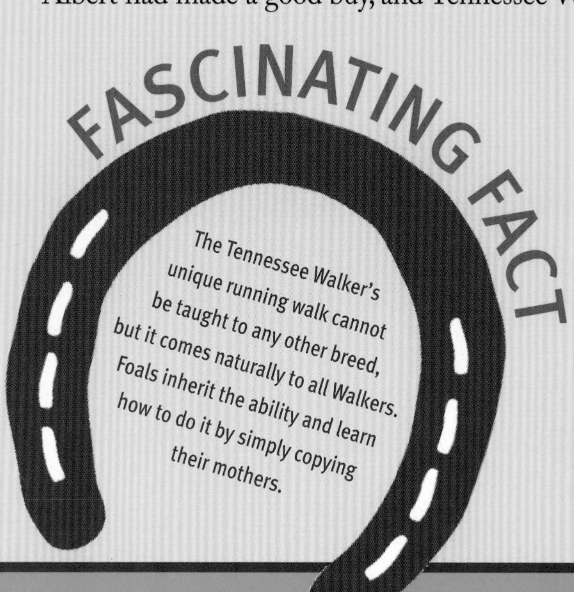

FASCINATING FACT

The Tennessee Walker's unique running walk cannot be taught to any other breed, but it comes naturally to all Walkers. Foals inherit the ability and learn how to do it by simply copying their mothers.

Skills

The Walker is a popular family and **pleasure horse**, and is ideal for **trail riding**. It is also a star in the show ring and, although mainly shown under saddle (with a rider), it is also shown **in harness** (driven, pulling a cart).

Thoroughbred

Thoroughbred

Vital statistics

Height: 16–16.2 hands, but can be as small as 14.2 or as big as 17.3!
Color: black, brown, **bay**, **gray**, or **chestnut**; often with white markings on face and legs
Physique: noble head with a straight face and intelligent eye; long, arched neck, short, strong back, and well-muscled **hindquarters**; fine, silky coat and fine mane and tail; build varies according to **type** (e.g. racehorse, **hunter**, show jumper)

The Thoroughbred is the fastest and most valuable horse in the world. Because it is almost perfect physically and is a great athlete, it is often **crossed** with other breeds to give them some of the Thoroughbred's qualities, such as speed and elegance. Thoroughbreds are brave and willing, and have lots of stamina, but they can also be highly strung, and are sometimes difficult to handle.

Origins

The breed was developed in England in the 1600s and 1700s, when fast English mares were crossed with proud Arab and **Barb** stallions from Arabia and North Africa. All Thoroughbreds are descended from three horses, called the "Byerley Turk," the "Darley Arabian," and the "Godolphin Arabian." Due to their speed, Thoroughbreds were bred for racing and are sometimes also known as "racehorses." They became popular in France and in the United States, which now breeds its own fine American Thoroughbreds.

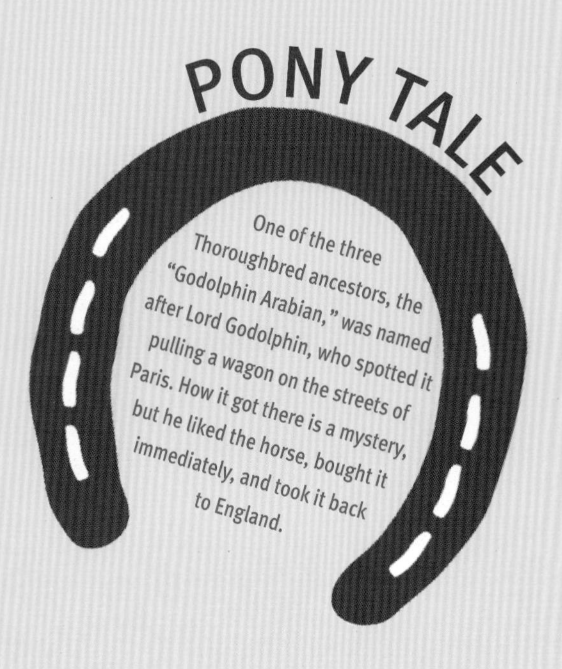

Skills

Although they are probably most famous as racehorses, Thoroughbreds are also excellent jumpers. When crossed with other breeds, they produce wonderful **pleasure horses** and **hunters**, and excellent show horses. They are also good at **dressage** and make great three-day **eventers**.

Trakehner

Vital statistics

Height: 16–17.2 hands

Color: any **solid color** but usually, **gray**, brown, or **chestnut**

Physique: small, tapering head with a broad forehead, intelligent eye, and long ears; long, strong neck, medium-long back, and powerful **hindquarters**; strong, slender legs and **hard feet**

Trakehners are good-natured and willing to work hard, but they can sometimes be a bit of a handful. As well as being extremely good-looking, they are naturally athletic and very graceful—they have a lovely, floating trot and a beautifully balanced canter. They have lots of stamina too, and do well at most horse disciplines. Today, the Trakehner is one of the best of the German breeds, but it is also found all over the world, and competes in the show ring at international level.

Origins

The Trakehner was first bred in 1732 at the famous **stud** farm at Trakehnen, East Prussia, now part of Poland. In the 1800s, Trakehners were **crossed** with Thoroughbreds to increase their size, and to give them spirit and stamina. The idea was to create a horse that could be used not only as a farm horse, but also as a cavalry horse for war. The Trakehner was later improved by the addition of Arab blood.

Skills

The Trakehner is a good all-rounder and makes a great competition horse. It is bold across country, jumping fences and ditches without the slightest hesitation, but its elegant movements make it a top **dressage** horse. Its powerful hindquarters are a real plus when it comes to show jumping, and it is a regular competitor at the Olympic Games. The German-bred stallion, "Abdullah," won gold and silver medals at the 1984 Olympics.

Welsh Pony

Vital statistics

Height: 12–13.2 hands
Color: usually **gray**, but can be any color except **piebald** or **skewbald**
Physique: small, Arab-type head with a slightly curved-in (**dished**) face and small, pointed ears; graceful neck, short, muscular back, and rounded **hindquarters**; strong legs and **hard feet**; tail carried high

The Welsh Pony comes from Britain and is intelligent, high-spirited, and energetic. It was developed from the Welsh Mountain Pony and has the same character and temperament, but the slightly larger Welsh Pony can do more than its mountain cousin, which never grows to more than 12 hands high. The Welsh Pony loves to compete in shows, and its kind nature makes it an excellent pony for children to ride and enter their first competitions.

Origins

The first Welsh Ponies were produced by **crossing** small Welsh Cobs with Welsh Mountain Ponies. They were then crossed with other breeds, including Arabs, **Barbs**, and Thoroughbreds. One of the Thoroughbred stallions was called "Merlin." He was allowed to run wild on the Welsh hills in the early 1800s and thanks to him Welsh Ponies are still sometimes called "Merlins."

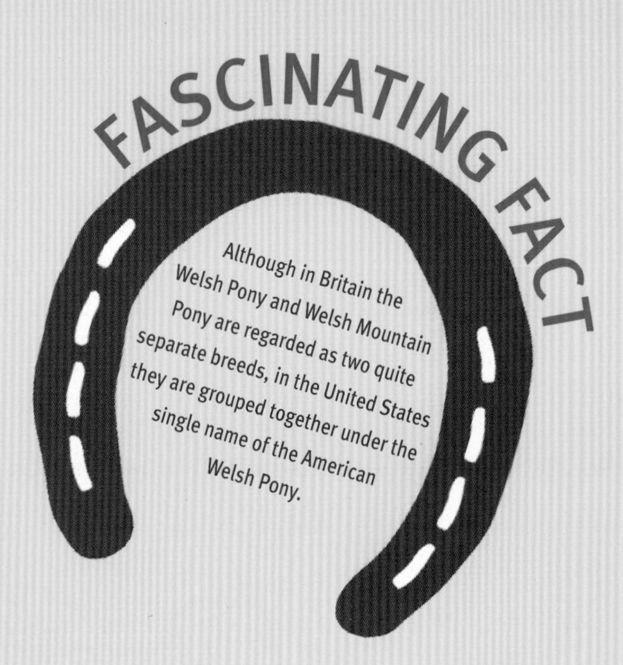

Skills

Welsh Ponies have kind natures and good temperaments. They love to be where the action is and make good children's ponies. They move well and elegantly, and, thanks to their courage, are bold jumpers. They are popular in the show ring, where they compete in events both carrying riders and **in harness**.

Glossary

Barb: a hardy, even-tempered horse originally from Morocco and Algeria, often used to improve other breeds.
Bay: a color that ranges from dark reddish brown to yellowish chestnut. Bay horses have a black mane and tail.
Broken (in): a horse that has been trained to work in a saddle and bridle, or in harness.
Buckskin: a light color, slightly darker than cream. Known as dun in Britain.
Chestnut: deep reddish-brown or golden-brown color.
Cow horse/pony: a horse or pony used to herd and rope cattle.
Cross-breed/crossing: to mate pure-bred horses of different breeds, usually to improve the breed of the cross (the new horse that is produced) by giving it the qualities of the parent breeds.
Cross(es): a horse or horses produced by cross-breeding (see above).
Dished: describes a face that is slightly curved inward below the eyes.
Dock: the fleshy part of the tail on which the hair grows.
Draft horse: a large, muscular horse used for pulling wagons and plows, for forestry and farm work.
Dressage: a test in which horse and rider perform a series of movements to show they have reached a high level of training.
Endurance: a competition, ridden for long distances over rough ground, that tests the stamina of horse and rider.
Eventer: a horse that is used for one-, two- or three-day events (dressage, cross-country, show jumping).
Feathers: a fringe of hair on the lower leg that covers the top part of the hoof, found in draft horses and some heavier breeds.
Gaited: a horse that uses unusual **gaits** (paces) as well as, or instead of, the usual walk, trot, and canter. In some breeds these gaits (paces) come naturally, in others they have to be learned.
Gray: different mixtures of black and white hairs that produce coat colors ranging from almost white to really dark (iron) gray.
Hand: horses are measured in hands—1 hand = 4 inches (10 cm)—from the top of the withers. In Europe, horses are also measured in meters and centimeters.
Hard (feet): hooves that are hard and strong and may not need the protection of horseshoes.
High school: advanced dressage and horse skills. High-school movements are very difficult to perform.
Hock: the joint connecting the upper and lower part of the horse's back leg.
Hindquarters: the rounded part at the back of the horse, above the hind (back) legs.
Hunter: see Type—a horse bred for hunting with hounds. Heavy hunters are good for land that is "heavy going" (mud and plowed fields), lighter weight hunters are faster across grassland.
(In) harness: the equipment (bridle, collar, reins) used for driving a horse, i.e. a horse pulling a cart or wagon. A horse in harness is being driven.
Pack animal: a pony or horse used for carrying heavy loads.
Palomino: a color that ranges from pale to bright gold, with a flaxen (almost white) mane and tail.
Piebald: a horse with large patches of black and white color.
Pleasure horse: a comfortable, well-mannered riding horse.
Points: refers to the color of the mane, tail, and lower part of the legs, e.g. a bay with black points.
Pony: a small horse up to 14.2 hands. This doesn't apply to some breeds, for example a polo pony is always a "pony" and an Arab is always a "horse" no matter what their height.
Roan: a mixture of light and dark hairs that gives the coat a speckled appearance—e.g. blue roan (black and white hairs), red or strawberry roan (brown/red and white hairs).
Saddle horse: a riding horse.
Skewbald: a horse with large patches of brown and white color.
Solid color: a horse that is a single color (bay, chestnut, buckskin, gray) and not a mixture.
Sorrel: a lighter red or golden chestnut horse, often with a lighter colored mane and tail.
Stud: a place (usually a farm) for breeding horses.
Trail riding: rides across country. The distances can vary. Usually known as trekking in Britain.
Type: tells you what a horse is used for. Examples of types are hunter, show jumper, draft horse, etc.
Withers: the top of a horse's shoulder, at the point where the neck meets the back.

Quercus
Smith-Davies Publishing plc
46 Dorset Street
London
W1U 7NB

First published 2006

Written by: Wendy Allatson
Proofread by: Lin Thomas
Design: Neal Cobourne
Editorial and project management: JMS Books LLP

A catalog record for this book is available from the British Library.

ISBN 1 905204 24 8

Printed in China